Rocky Top Middle School
14150 York St.
Thornton, CO 806

Divorce
Finding a Place

by Eileen Kuehn

Consultant:
Roderick W. Franks, MA, LSW
Licensed Psychologist
Hennepin County Family Court Services
Minneapolis, Minnesota

Grief and Loss

LifeMatters
an imprint of Capstone Press
Mankato, Minnesota

LifeMatters Books are published by Capstone Press
PO Box 669 • 151 Good Counsel Drive • Mankato, Minnesota 56002
http://www.capstone-press.com

Printed in the United States of America

Library of Congress Cataloging-in-Publication Data
Kuehn, Eileen.
      Divorce: finding a place / by Eileen Kuehn.
          p.   cm. — (Grief and loss)
      Includes bibliographical references and index.
      ISBN 0-7368-0747-0
      1. Children of divorced parents—United States—Psychology—Juvenile literature. 2. Teenagers—United States—Psychology—Juvenile literature. 3. Teenagers—United States—Life skills guides—Juvenile literature. 4. Divorce—United States—Juvenile literature. [1. Divorce.] I. Title. II. Series.
      HQ777.5 .K84 2001
      155.44—dc21   00-010134
                                               CIP

      Summary: Defines divorce and its effect on teens. Provides ideas for coping with divorce, returning to a normal life, and helping other teens who may experience a divorce.

Staff Credits
Charles Pederson, editor; Adam Lazar, designer; Kim Danger, photo researcher

Photo Credits
Cover: UPmagazine/©Tim Yoon
Index Stock Photography, 51
International Stock/©Jeff Greenberg, 9; ©Scott Barrow, 13; ©Mark Bolster, 19; ©Giovanni Lunardi, 26; ©Mark Bolster, 31; ©Patric Ramsey, 36, 40; ©Richard Dean, 49
Photo Network/©Tom McCarthy, 6, 34
Uniphoto, 58/©Bob Daemmrich Photos, 16, 57; ©Terry Wild, 47
UPmagazine/©Tim Yoon, 59

Table of Contents

○ Divorce is a legal process that ends a marriage. It's also a time of major change for families.

○ People get divorced for many reasons. Divorce often happens because two married people can't agree on issues. It may occur because people change and grow apart. It may occur for many other reasons.

○ Experts have identified three stages in a divorce. The first stage is a temporary crisis period when parents initially separate. The second stage is when legal issues usually are resolved. The last stage can take several years. It's the time needed to get through the changes that the divorce causes.

○ Divorce can have a big effect on teens. It can cause feelings of shame, guilt, anger, fear, denial, and depression. These feelings can affect a teen's life in many ways.

Chapter 1

What Is Divorce?

Defining Divorce

In its most basic sense, divorce is a legal process that ends a marriage. However, it's also much more. It's a cause of major change for families. Divorce is hard, but it's not impossible to deal with.

A divorce occurs when a husband and wife decide they no longer want to be married. They go through a legal process to end the marriage officially. Many divorces happen quickly. However, the process can take a long time. Some divorces take a year or more before they're final. Divorce sometimes can be simple and inexpensive. Other times, it can involve two or more lawyers, many documents, and lots of money.

Sometimes the issues related to a divorce are contested. A contested divorce occurs when parents can't agree on custody of children and division of property. In a contested divorce, a judge decides who is responsible for the children and how to divide property. When divorcing people agree about custody and property, it's an uncontested divorce.

Other times, a trained problem solver called a mediator helps parents talk through issues. Parents then make their own decisions about custody and about dividing their property. With mediation, the divorce process usually doesn't go to trial.

Either way, if there are children, the couple must settle issues such as custody and child support. This is money one parent pays the other to help support children. In some cases, one parent may make spousal maintenance payments. Spousal maintenance is sometimes called alimony. This is money one spouse pays to support the other. Sometimes a parent must pay both child support and spousal maintenance. This is especially true if the custodial parent doesn't work much or at all outside the home.

Causes of Divorce

People get divorced for many reasons. Parents may no longer love each other. They may physically or emotionally abuse or mistreat each other or the children. Parents may love and want to live with another person. They may disagree on important family issues, such as how to spend their money or where to live.

Sometimes a divorce happens after parents fight a lot. Suddenly, one parent may decide to leave the family. Other times, a divorce happens quietly over a longer time. An unhappy parent may find excuses to stay away from home. Then he or she may just stop coming home at all. Parents may begin to do more and more things separately. For example, maybe they begin to take separate vacations after taking them together for many years.

Did You Know?

During and after a divorce, teens can have difficulty adjusting to changes. Experts say that most children of divorce experience a short period of upset and confusion. During this time, they need strong emotional support from friends and adults. Their life needs a clear structure. For example, having schedules for doing homework or for visiting a noncustodial parent can be helpful.

Stages of Divorce

Divorce can be divided into three stages. The length of each stage varies by family and individual. However, most families go through all stages at one time or another.

The first stage is a crisis period that can last from two months to two years. It's when parents first are separated. Usually, one parent moves out. This is called a crisis period because it seems like the household is turned upside down. The parents' decision to get divorced surprises many children of divorce. Generally, children aren't prepared for the changes to come.

The second stage lasts from six months to a few years. It's the time when the legal process concludes and a judge grants the divorce. Conflict and lack of cooperation between parents can continue during this stage. Parents may continue to fight in court about custody and property issues. They also may turn to their children for emotional support and comfort during this time. One parent may try to turn the children against the other parent.

At a Glance

Parents can help children through a divorce by:

- Explaining what's going to happen and why

- Reassuring them that they didn't cause the divorce and that both parents still love them

- Making sure they understand they can't do anything about the divorce

- Explaining that there's no possibility of the parents getting back together

The third stage usually lasts two to three years after the initial separation. Parents may stop fighting outwardly but may continue to have bad feelings beneath the surface. These feelings can be a source of major stress for children of divorced parents. Stress also comes from the absence of the noncustodial parent. Parental dating and remarriage can be upsetting. These stresses can cause communication barriers between parents and children that may last for years after a divorce.

Michael, Age 17

Michael is the oldest of three children. His parents divorced when he was 13. For him, the divorce meant lots of change. It broke up his family. He doesn't see his dad anymore.

At first he felt really angry at both parents, but that didn't last long. Now he considers the divorce part of life.

Effects of Divorce

As it did for Michael's family, divorce changes how a family lives. It may change where teens go to school. It probably will change where at least one parent lives.

These changes cause some teens to feel sad, hopeless, or lonely. These are perfectly normal feelings. Other feelings teens may have include embarrassment, shame, guilt, anger, fear, denial, and depression. Teens also may have conflicting emotions.

Embarrassment or Shame

After a divorce, teens may feel ashamed. They might feel that they've done something wrong. They also may be embarrassed. For example, their parents may fight in front of other people. The teens may be embarrassed to talk about the divorce with their friends or other people.

Guilt

Teens often feel guilty about the divorce. They may feel they did something that caused their parents to split. Many things can cause divorce, but children don't. Sometimes parents may claim their children caused a divorce. However, the parents really may mean that they didn't want the responsibility of raising children. It can take years, even into adulthood, for a child of divorce to deal with guilt.

Cher, Age 14

Cher asked her parents if she could go to a rock concert with her friends one weekend. Cher's father was willing, but her mother said, "You're too young. You have to wait another year or two." Cher got angry and screamed, "I hate you both. I wish you were both gone!"

Two months later, her parents told her they were getting divorced. Cher blamed herself. "Maybe they fought about me," she thought. She was afraid that losing her temper about the concert caused her parents to get divorced.

Anger

When teens blame themselves for a divorce, they may get angry with themselves. They also may get angry at their parents and fight with them. They may direct their anger at brothers, sisters, or friends. The anger comes from feeling hurt about what has happened. It also can be a way to hide sadness and fear. It's important to recognize and deal with anger as soon as possible.

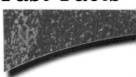

- The divorce rate doubled between 1960 and 1975. By the late 1990s, there were more than 1 million divorces each year.

- About 80 percent of men and 75 percent of women remarry within three years of their divorce. About 60 percent of those new marriages end in divorce.

Fear

Because divorce brings change and uncertainty, it's easy to be afraid of many things. Teens may think that because their parents stopped loving each other, they'll stop loving the children, too. They may fear that both parents will leave them. They may fear they'll lose their friends. They may think people will avoid them. Children of divorce may fear they'll have to move away from friends and school. They may be afraid there won't be enough money.

Denial

Teens often deny to themselves and others what happened. This denial may cause teens not to accept a divorce. They may hope their parents will get back together. They might dream of being one family again. They may want to believe the divorce can be fixed and that life will be as it was. Children of divorce may try to get their parents to spend more time together.

Teen Talk

Depression

It's upsetting to see parents fight and split. This can lead to depression. Depression is a mood disorder that causes great sadness and hopelessness. Teens can feel so sad and hopeless they withdraw from life. They may even stop eating or sleeping. They may take unusual health risks such as using and abusing alcohol or other drugs. Taking health risks seems to numb some people's feelings. Signs of depression are:

- Lack of interest in things once enjoyed

- Deep sadness or excessive crying

- Feelings of helplessness, hopelessness, guilt, or poor self-esteem

- Withdrawal from friends and family

- Difficulty concentrating or making decisions

- Eating too little or too much

- Thoughts about suicide, or killing yourself

If you or friends have any of these feelings, talk with a trusted adult right away. You may even want to talk with a professional counselor or therapist. This person can help you sort through these feelings before they become overwhelming.

Conflicting Emotions

Divorce can cause conflicting emotions in teens. They may want their parents to stay together *and* to split up. They may feel insecure and worry about what will happen to them. They may want to leave home and be on their own.

Each person facing a divorce has different feelings. All of these feelings are normal. People can learn to deal with their feelings in helpful ways.

Points to Consider

- Do you know anyone whose parents are divorced? How do you feel about that person? Explain.

- What would you say to a friend who told you he thought he caused his parents' divorce?

- If you're not from a divorced family, do you ever wonder if divorce might happen to you? Why or why not?

- When parents decide to divorce, they also must decide other issues such as custody and visitation.

- These decisions can produce big changes for a teen whose parents are divorcing. It can change living arrangements or relationships with family and friends. It also can cause changes in school.

- After a divorce, teens may have feelings of low self-esteem. If this happens, they need to find trusted adults they can talk with.

- Parents can help teens deal with divorce by knowing when to offer support or when to leave them alone. Either way, it's important to keep the communication lines open.

Chapter 2

What Happens After the Divorce Is Final?

Roxanne, Age 13

Her parents didn't spend much time together before the divorce. Still, Roxanne didn't like how her mother treated her father afterward.

One day when she was angry, Roxanne screamed at her mother, "You treat Dad like he was never here. You burned all his photos. You talk about him in bad ways in front of us. We don't like it!"

Roxanne's mother looked surprised and sad. "I'm sorry I hurt your feelings," she said.

What Happens After Divorce

Many things are uncertain after a divorce. The one sure thing is that it will bring change. Some changes are small, others may be big. Removing pictures from a wall is a small change. Having a parent leave is big. Both small and big changes can cause strong feelings.

Divorce can have good and bad points. On the positive side, it can mean an end to emotional or physical pain. It also can mean the beginning of a new, happier life. On the downside, it can mean confusion and depression. There may be less money for the family and emotional or behavioral problems for teens.

From 1900 until recently, judges usually awarded custody of a couple's children to the mother. Fathers were thought of as the main income earners with no big role in bringing up the children. This has changed. In the last 15 years, custody usually has been based on the best interests of the children.

Custody and Child Support

Once the divorce is final, the custody plan goes into effect. A judge and parents together usually decide custody arrangements. Sometimes just one parent has custody. Other times, parents may share custody equally. Custody plans can take several forms:

- **Joint custody:** Child lives part-time with each parent.

- **Sole custody:** Child lives full-time with one parent.

- **Split custody:** One parent takes care of some of the children, and the other parent takes care of any others.

- **Third-party custody:** Child lives with someone other than the parents.

The judge also decides about child support. If a teen lives with one parent, the other parent probably will be required to pay child support.

At a Glance

Here are some tips to help make going between two households easier:

1. Get organized and know what you need in each place. A checklist can be helpful.

2. Ask your parents for a weekly written schedule of where you will be and when.

3. Make a central spot in your room. Use it for all the things you normally carry back and forth between your two homes.

4. Have two sets of basic stuff—one set for each house. This could include a toothbrush, toothpaste, contact lens stuff, homework supplies, and so on.

Visitation

If one parent has custody, the other may have visitation rights. That means the noncustodial parent can visit the child on a schedule that everyone agrees to. Visits may be allowed once a week, once a year, or any other amount.

Barb, Age 14

Usually, Barb lives with her mother. Her older brother lives with her father. That was how the judge decided the custody arrangement. Her father doesn't like the decision. He wants Barb to live with him, too. Barb loves both of her parents, but she gets tired of traveling back and forth between their homes.

Two Households

If parents have joint custody, a teen will have two households. For example, Barb probably has two sets of clothes, rules, or friends. It can be hard to carry things back and forth between two homes. It might be hard to juggle two lives. You can feel like two separate people.

The juggling may become easier if you use lists of things to bring to and from each home. It also helps to list things to do at each home, such as household chores and homework. Parents may be able to help with this.

School Performance

School may seem less important after a divorce. Teens may not study because they're tired, stressed out, or unhappy. Sometimes it seems easier just to stay home. This may be easy if the custodial parent works outside the home.

If school performance starts to slide, it's time to seek help. Talk with a parent or teacher. It may be just a matter of time before school becomes fun and interesting again. Sometimes setting up a schedule to do homework can help teens stay focused. Studying with friends may help. So might talking with a professional who is trained to help children of divorce.

Teen Talk

"I'm sort of excited to live part-time with each of my parents. I get to pick out new bedroom furniture and decorate my room twice!" —Jane, age 13

"I don't get to see my dad as much as I used to before the divorce. But my parents have agreed on scheduled times for me to go see him."—Jacob, age 15

Family Relationships

After a divorce, family relationships may change. Family members may seem less patient with each other. Feelings may be hurt more easily. On the other hand, some families may become closer.

Teens may blame the parent who asked for the divorce. They may blame the other parent, believing he or she caused the divorce. They may think their parents didn't try hard enough to avoid it.

Families may feel closer together and farther apart at the same time. This is because family members are working together to recover from the divorce. At the same time, each person may be becoming more independent because of new responsibilities.

Sometimes parents have a hard time talking with their children about the divorce. They may feel guilty because the divorce hurts their children. They may feel embarrassed at thinking they failed in the marriage. This is a time when children can help their parents by being patient and understanding. It's also helpful for everyone to cooperate. It's a hard time for everyone.

Relationships With Friends

After a divorce, friendships may change, especially if a family has to move. A teen may split time between two households and see friends less often. A person may avoid friends who seem uncomfortable around him or her. Friends may feel that anything they say will be wrong. Or they may think their friend doesn't want to talk about the divorce.

Self-Esteem

Divorce often makes teens feel they're not worthwhile. They may think they caused the divorce by doing something wrong. Moving to a smaller house or having less money also may lower self-esteem. These feelings are common.

Losing self-esteem can be gradual. Ask yourself these questions to check out your feelings:

- Am I doing as well in school as I can?

- Do I have good relationships with my friends?

- Are my family relationships good?

- Do I stay out of trouble with school and legal authorities?

If the answer to any of these questions is no, it might be time to talk with a professional counselor. Such professional problem solvers can be found through parents, school, a place of worship, or a trusted adult.

Did You Know?

Experts say there's less stress between parents if they go through conflict resolution training before or during a divorce. Conflict resolution is a way to work through challenges without fighting. It can be learned from professionals in classes or in one-to-one training sessions.

How Parents Can Help

Parents can help teens deal with divorce by being sensitive to their needs. Some teens may want to talk about the divorce. Some may not. Sometimes communication happens without words. Holding hands, giving a hug, or even a smile may help another person feel better. Parents also can help by knowing when to leave teens alone.

The doors to communication can best be kept open when teens let parents know what they need. A direct, honest statement like "I can't talk about it now" is a good approach. Then a parent can answer, "I'll be ready when you do want to talk about it." Sometimes talking about other things can bring up the topic of feelings that the divorce causes.

Here are some other helpful things parents can tell teens during a divorce:

- Parents may not love each other anymore, but they still love their children

- Where the children are going to live

- How often children will see their parents

- Why their parents are splitting

- That it wasn't the teen's fault

Points to Consider

- If your parents are divorced, think of how you feel about it. What could you do to feel better?

- Do you think a divorce might be positive? Why or why not?

- Would you feel comfortable telling your parents you need time to be alone?

- List three things you could do to make a smoother switch between households.

O Teens react to divorce in different ways, depending on their age. Understanding these behaviors can help teens be more supportive of brothers and sisters. They may find that helping others is a way to help themselves.

O Sometimes the stress of divorce pushes a teen into using drugs or alcohol. Teens also may experience other behavioral or emotional challenges.

O Teens of divorce may suffer deeply from loss if they see a parent less after a divorce.

O Divorce can cause other changes if parents start dating other people. Major adjustments may be needed if a parent remarries.

Chapter 3

How Divorce Affects Your Life

Reactions to Divorce

Kids of all ages share common reactions to divorce, such as those discussed in Chapter 1. Kids also react in unique ways depending on age. Very young children may have no memories of the family before the divorce. Living with a single parent may be all they know. Older children and teens may have vivid memories of the past.

It's helpful for teens to understand how divorce may affect people at different ages. They may be able to help others. Helping others also may help the teen.

Preschool Children

Preschool children haven't yet had many life experiences. Having
a parent move out can be confusing and upsetting. They may feel
abandoned by that parent and be afraid the other parent will leave,
too. Children this age often believe the divorce happened because
of them. They may feel sad and cry a lot but not understand why.
Formerly secure preschool children may become demanding or
clingy after the divorce.

Children and Preteens (Ages 5–12)

Children this age know what divorce means. They may feel
abandoned and insecure, as well as angry and resentful. Children
and preteens may fear that something will happen to the parent
they live with. They may feel deep shame or loneliness. They also
might think they caused their parents to split up. Children this age
may feel they must take sides with one parent. They also may
have changes at school and with friends.

Divorce

Here are some warning signs that a divorce is causing too much stress for a teen:

- Feeling depressed, ill, or tired

- Abusing substances such as alcohol or other drugs

- Injuring oneself through carelessness or on purpose

- Getting into trouble with the law or at school

- Running away from home

Young Teens (Ages 13–15)

At this age, a divorce may cause extreme stress. Young teens already experience many physical, social, and emotional changes. Young teens often feel confused, moody, and insecure. They may use childlike behaviors such as being clingy or demanding.

They may reject parents and get overly attached to friends or a pet. They themselves may feel rejected and ashamed. They may have problems with sleeping, health, school, or friends. They may be angry at one or both parents. However, this anger may hide their real feelings of sadness, depression, and helplessness.

Older Teens (Ages 16–18)

Older teens are trying to establish their own identity. Divorce may push them to feel independent before they really are. Their circumstances may overwhelm them and feel unsolvable. It can be hard to concentrate. Teens may feel tired. They may test their parents' love by misbehaving or getting angry with them. They may resent their parents' dating others.

Alcohol and Other Drugs

Sometimes teens are so unhappy about a divorce that they turn to alcohol and other drugs. They may think these substances will help stop the pain. They may believe drinking or using drugs will help them make friends in a new school or neighborhood. However, using alcohol or other drugs creates more problems than it solves.

Other Emotional Struggles

In rare cases, a teen can become violently angry about the divorce. This may cause him or her to get into trouble with parents or even police.

It's important to talk with someone about these feelings right away. Talk with a family member, close friend, or teacher. Find ways to ease pain and tension before it gets too hard to deal with.

Lorenzo, Age 15

One day Lorenzo's parents were arguing loudly in the kitchen. Lorenzo walked into the kitchen. His parents seemed surprised that he had heard them. "Are you guys getting divorced?" he asked.

"Absolutely not," his mother said, giving him a hug. "We'd never do that to you." His father agreed.

A year later, his parents divorced. His dad moved to a new state. It made Lorenzo mad because they'd lied to him about it. He no longer felt he could trust anything his parents said.

Divorce

- The absence of a father after divorce is common. Over one-third of all children whose parents divorce experience the loss of their father.

- Many children whose father leaves after divorce perform worse academically and socially than children with an available father. They may get lower grades, score lower on achievement tests, and miss more school.

When You Can't See Your Parent

Either parent may leave a family of divorce without saying good-bye. A parent may leave because he or she can't afford to support the kids financially. A parent may move far away and find it hard to stay involved with the children. A parent may feel too much anger and bitterness to say good-bye. Or the custodial parent may not allow the other parent to visit. A parent also may be absent because he or she starts a new family. After leaving, a parent may not talk with the children for long periods of time.

No matter the reason, a parent's absence hurts. Children are likely to feel rejected and unloved. They may have low self-esteem because they blame themselves for the absence. Or they may blame the remaining parent.

When a parent drops out of a child's life, it's often because that parent has problems, too. The best solution is for the family to pull together and support each other. Doing activities together can help. Talking about feelings also can help.

How to Talk About It

Teens may find it hard to talk about a divorce. They may be afraid of how others will react. They may mistakenly believe that no one else has such terrible problems.

Teen Talk

"I think my parents' divorce was actually good for our family. The fighting stopped. They both seem happier. They can build new lives for themselves and us kids."—Mary Lou, age 17

"I was shocked when my parents got divorced. They'd been fighting for a long time, and we'd gotten used to it. But when the divorce finally happened—man, it was stressful."—Mark, age 15

The easiest way to talk about divorce is to be honest about feelings. Tell the truth. Talking with a trusted adult is often a good first step. It also may help to talk with a close friend.

Tanya, Age 13

"I hope you're not going out with that creepy Chuck again," Tanya said to her mother angrily one Friday night. Her mom was getting ready to go out.

"It's none of your business, dear," her mother said.

"It will be my business if you ever bring him home," Tanya threatened. She ran from the room before her mother could see her cry.

Tanya doesn't like her mom dating other men since her parents' divorce. She hates to think about the possibility of her mom remarrying. The last thing she wants is some man trying to pretend he's her father. She believes that dating takes her mom away from her. She sees her mom so little now, anyway.

Parents Who Date

After a divorce, one or both parents might start dating again. This can be a strange experience for the teens. On one hand, teens want their parents to be happy. On the other hand, teens may feel disloyal to one or both parents. They may not like the person their parent is dating. They may like the person but don't want to be disappointed if the relationship doesn't work out.

If parents do start to date, it's important to be polite to the friend. It helps to have an open mind. Teens should be honest with their parents about their feelings on dating. It also helps teens to have other things to occupy them, such as hobbies.

Points to Consider

- Say you had a friend whose parents are divorced. How might you help that friend avoid alcohol or other drugs?

- How might a 9-year-old be able to handle divorce differently from a 14-year-old?

- Do you think it's better or worse if a mother rather than a father is absent after a divorce? Explain.

⦿ The emotions that happen after a divorce can be hard to understand. There are ways to cope with these emotions.

⦿ A divorce can cause teens to take on more responsibility in the family. It also can cause them to grow up too fast.

⦿ Sometimes parents continue to fight with each other after a divorce. They also may be too busy to spend much time with their teens.

⦿ Teens and parents need to communicate when coping with divorce.

Ideas for Coping With Divorce

Chapter 4

Wanda, Age 16

About six months after her parents' divorce, Wanda noticed her big brother, Ed, writing in a notebook. "What are you writing?" she asked him.

"Just some thoughts about why I felt so low yesterday," he said.

Wanda thought this seemed like a good idea. She wrote in her own journal whenever she got sad about the divorce or other things. Sometimes she wrote about silly things to get her mind off the divorce. She started writing poems. One of them even got published in her school's literary journal. She and her parents felt proud.

Coping Emotionally

Emotions can be hard to understand at any time but they are especially difficult after a divorce. Sometimes the feelings come out of nowhere and make no sense. Don't keep feelings inside. It's better to talk or cry. Reach out to friends or family. Remember, it's okay to feel bad. Laughing also helps, even if you laugh at yourself. Here are some other ways to cope with emotions:

- Write about your feelings in a notebook, in a journal, or on a computer.

- Listen to music or play an instrument.

- Find a special place to think, read, or write.

- Develop a hobby.

- Think about your future.

"Being able to talk openly with Mom and Dad makes me feel like I'm not alone. It's a relief."—Sandra, age 16

"I told my parents to settle their issues alone and not in front of me or my sisters. We just couldn't handle any more stress. They've been pretty good about it since then."—Warren, age 17

- Imagine the kind of marriage and family you want as an adult.

- Talk with your family or friends.

- Confide in your brothers and sisters.

- Keep physically active.

Coping Physically

It's important to be healthy when life becomes stressful. Staying fit increases a person's energy level and helps keep away illnesses such as colds and flu. It can help avoid depression, which is a common reaction to divorce. Here are some ways to stay healthy:

- Exercise every day.

- Go out for a sport at school or in your community.

- Get involved in community activities.

- Get plenty of sleep.

- Don't get overinvolved in activities and get burned out.

- Eat healthy meals three times a day.

Coping Socially

Friends can offer valuable support when coping with a divorce. These may be old or new friends. Moving to a new neighborhood can be scary. However, a change of surroundings sometimes can help you make a fresh start. Attending parties or sports events can help, too, just to get your mind off your situation.

Sometimes making friends can be hard. But probably this is only temporary. If it's difficult for you to make new friends, you still can find people to be with. You might try these things:

- Visit grandparents, uncles, and aunts.

- Look for an old friend to talk with.

- Find adults who will listen.

- Join a divorce support group for teens.

- Join youth activities at your school or place of worship.

- Find other teens who share your interests.

It's expected that soon there will be more stepfamilies than natural families in the United States.

Aliyah, Age 16

Since the divorce, Aliyah felt more grown-up. She felt like she could conquer the world. She took on more responsibility around the house. She took care of her little sister while her mom worked. Aliyah didn't feel like a kid anymore.

The bad thing was that Aliyah lost respect for her mom. Aliyah thought she should be able to stay out late because she did so much work at home.

Growing Up Too Fast

After a divorce, family roles can change. Teens may take on more responsibility such as getting a job. Sometimes older children act like parents to younger brothers and sisters. Parents may rely on their teens more or turn to them for companionship.

Even though a teen thinks and acts more mature, most teens still need an adult's guidance. Teens and parents may have to work together to establish reasonable guidelines for behavior. For example, they may agree to curfews for the teens to be home.

At a Glance

How to keep your relationship with parents strong even when they work or are far away:

- Send e-mail messages.

- Leave messages on answering machines.

- Send postcards and letters.

- Make them an audiotape or videotape.

- Write them a story or poem.

When Parents Are Busy

Sometimes parents don't have as much time for their children after a divorce as they did before. If this happens, talk with them about it. Set up a regular date to do something together. Try to make your time together special.

If a parent is busy, be patient and persistent. Meanwhile, seek out other people to spend time with. This could be grandparents, aunts, uncles, or cousins. Do things with friends or neighbors.

The Importance of Communication

If parents continue to fight after a divorce, everything is more confusing. Teens can leave the room if parents fight in front of them. Or teens may suggest that their parents get counseling. It's unfair if parents expect teens to take the side of one parent against the other. If this happens, teens have the right to tell their parents they don't want to take sides.

Both children and parents need to express themselves when coping with divorce. Telling each other what you need is the best way. For example, leave notes or letters if it's too hard to talk. Don't keep your feelings bottled up inside.

"I had a hard time telling my parents how much their fighting bothered me. Finally, I wrote down some words from my favorite song that described my feelings. I gave the words to my parents. That opened the door to a good discussion."
—Maya, age 15

One way to explain your needs to parents is to create a teen's Bill of Rights. This document explains your feelings and expectations. Create this document with your parents' help. Ask your parents to help you to live by it. They may not agree to it, but at least they'll know how you feel. Here's an example of a Bill of Rights.

- I have the right to spend time alone with each of my parents.

- I have the right to expect my parents to tell the truth and not break promises or lie.

- I have the right to tell parents not to fight in front of me because it scares and worries me.

- I have the right to ask for help with homework.

- I have the right to want my parents to share important information with me.

- I have the right to expect my parents to listen and pay attention to me.

Consider creating a Bill of Rights about the divorce. It might help you and your parents understand each other better.

- I have the right to expect my parents not to take their feelings out on me. This is true even if they're angry, sad, depressed, or stressed.

- I have the right to communicate my feelings at any time.

- I have the right not to express my feelings if I don't want to.

- I have the right not to say bad things to one parent about the other.

- I have the right not to feel guilty about loving both parents.

- I have the right to schedules I can count on.

- I have the right to stay out of arguments between parents.

Divorce

Only about one-fourth to one-third of parents who divorce have a cooperative relationship with each other.

Points to Consider

- Do you feel that you can talk with friends and family about divorce?

- Do you feel healthy and strong enough to deal with the stresses of a divorce? Explain.

- Name three things you do that help you cope with difficult situations. Explain how they help you.

- How might divorce be different for an only child than for a child with brothers and sisters?

- Children of divorce may fear the future. They have learned that nothing is certain.

- The first two years after a divorce are often the hardest. After that, life usually evens out, though it can be a struggle.

- Children of divorce can take care of themselves by staying healthy, active, and focused on life. Attending support groups can help in recovery.

- Feelings of sadness and depression may last for years after a divorce. This may be especially true on holidays and special occasions.

- A parent's remarriage can be hard. Living in a blended family requires understanding and sensitivity. However, there are many ways to live happily with new family members.

Chapter 5

The Road to Recovery

Chapter 4 discussed ways to cope with divorce. Once you get past the coping point, it's time to start looking toward the future. Then the effect and power of the memories of the divorce can begin to fade.

Lucy and Nate, Ages 16 and 17

Lucy and Nate have been friends for years. Recently they became closer when both went through a divorce. Walking home from school, they often talked about it.

Lucy said, "One thing worries me most. I won't be able to invite my dad to my wedding if I ever get married. I'm not sure my mom and dad could be in the same room without fighting!"

Nate said, "My parents get along okay. I don't even think much about their divorce anymore. But I'm really worried about college. I wish I had paid more attention to my grades. I'm not sure I'll get a scholarship."

Did You Know?

Support groups and organizations can help families going through divorce. They can:

- Reduce parental conflict

- Create a new relationship with divorced parents

- Help teens grieve

- Improve parent-child relationships

- Promote successful stepparenting

Check pages 60–61 for ideas of where to look. Ask an adult you trust to recommend a group.

Teens of divorce tend to worry more about the future than other kids. The divorce has taught them that nothing is certain in life. As they look toward the future, they may become afraid. It's normal to feel overwhelmed about the future. Questions like "Will my parents get along at my wedding?" and "How will I pay for college?" are natural.

How Long Does It Take?

Most teens who've gone through a divorce say the first two years are the hardest. After that, they often get involved in their new life and begin to feel happy again. However, the struggle to stay happy continues.

Challenges may continue after a divorce if one parent is absent. Some challenges can occur if a parent remarries and the stepparent and teen don't have a good relationship. Watch for signs of distress at this time. Such signs include moodiness, angry outbursts, depression, and anxiety. If you notice any of these signs in yourself or others, seek help. One way is through a support group.

Support Group

← **Room 3B**

Erik, Age 15

"Are you going to Teen League tonight?" Erik asked Clyde.

"Yep, I'll be there. We're rehearsing for the talent show, right?" Clyde said.

They were going to lip-synch a pop song for their act. Erik was excited. Getting involved with guys in the same situation as his helped Erik feel better about his parents' divorce. He knows the divorce changed his life forever. But he also knows he can deal with it. The support group has helped him do that.

Support Groups

Sometimes going to a support group can help in recovering from the pain of a divorce. Erik found that out after his parents divorced. It was good to talk with people who were going through the same experiences. Right after his dad moved out, Erik joined a group that met twice a week. He felt he needed more help in the beginning. His current support group meets once a week.

Teen Talk

Many support groups exist for teens going through divorce. Churches, mosques, synagogues, or other religious institutions may have them. Schools also may have divorce support groups for teens. For More Information, on pages 60–61, can give you a starting place.

Divorcing parents often encourage their teens to attend a support group. Teens even can go on their own. Support groups can be a good, safe place to express feelings around people you trust. Support groups also can be fun and a place to develop friendships that can last a lifetime.

Taking Care of Yourself

It can be hard to work through a problem without the support of other people, but it's possible. One way is to stay focused on your own life. Keep active. Work on doing well in school. Set personal goals that will help you feel successful when you reach them. For example, say you've always wanted to run in a distance race. Now might be a good time to go for it!

Another way to take care of yourself is to talk to yourself about the divorce. In these talks, remind yourself of these things:

- The divorce wasn't your fault.

- Some good things have happened after the divorce. For example, you probably feel more relaxed at home.

- You've faced some challenges that have helped you grow stronger emotionally.

Backsliding

Your life since the divorce may be better than you thought it would be. Sometimes, however, sad feelings may creep back. This can happen for years after the divorce. That's normal. You may feel silly talking about those sad feelings long after the divorce. But talking about them is the right thing to do.

Sometimes a teen doesn't want to go through counseling right away when a divorce happens. A few years later, however, counseling may be just what's needed. By that time, a person may be more open to it. Divorce often has an effect on teens that can't be seen at the time it happens. Later, talking about and understanding certain challenges that resulted from divorce may be easier.

Teen Talk

"I feel especially sad about the divorce at holidays and birthdays. My parents pressure me to act happy. I have news for them. I'm not always happy."—Terry, age 17

Holidays and Special Occasions

Life after divorce can present many new issues. For example, family events may be different. It's hard when teens must split a holiday between parents. It's sad if one parent doesn't come to a birthday party or other family events.

It helps to think about these situations ahead of time. Develop a plan to handle them. Communicate these plans to parents. For example, you might suggest separate parties for each parent.

Patrick, Age 17

Patrick dreads Christmas. He always spends Christmas Eve with his mom and Christmas Day with his dad. This year is even harder because his dad's girlfriend is bringing her two kids for the day.

Patrick doubts his dad will remarry. But if he did, Patrick would probably feel bad about it. He thinks his dad's new wife and kids wouldn't accept him. He's afraid he'd feel like an outsider.

Parents Who Remarry

It may be difficult if parents remarry, blending two families into one. Teens may be afraid to like or love the new parent. They may feel guilty if they do. They may feel they're betraying their other parent. They also may fear that the new parent will leave someday.

If a parent marries someone with children, the new family must adjust to living together. This can cause good and bad feelings. Teens may feel pushed out by these new brothers or sisters. It can be scary if a new baby is born to the family.

Living in a Blended Family

Things won't always go smoothly in a blended family, but certain steps can make life easier. First, keep a positive attitude. Give the stepparent a chance. Maybe he or she is a good cook or good listener. Compliment the stepparent on the positive qualities you notice. Remember that living with you may be hard for the stepparent, too. Try to spend time together doing fun things. You may discover you enjoy being part of two families.

At a Glance

Blending two families can be both fun and challenging. It may seem strange at first, but it can be a good experience. Think of positive things about stepfamilies:

- A same-sex parent can be a good role model.

- It can be good to be a part of a new family.

- Two happily married parents can show teens that marriages can work.

- Remarriage can end worries about money.

- Stepbrothers or stepsisters can provide friendship and support.

Here are some other ways to deal with new family members:

- Get to know your new brothers or sisters. Ask them about themselves. Tell them about yourself. You may find they share some of your feelings.

- Think of what you don't like about your relationship. Then work to improve it.

- Do some activities with your new brothers or sisters. For example, join a sports team, take an after-school class, or go shopping together.

- Talk with your parent if you feel you don't fit in with the new family. Look for a solution together.

Is There Such a Thing as a Happy Marriage?

Teens of divorced parents likely will get married someday. But this decision can be scary to teens. They might find it hard to believe marriage really can work.

Many teens try to be extra careful not to repeat their parents' mistakes. This also can cause them to stay in a marriage long after it's not working. Other teens may be afraid to get married in the first place. They fear marriage can't last. These reactions are normal. But remember:

- Not everyone gets divorced.

- You can learn from your parents' mistakes.

- Adults whose marriages have lasted are good sources of encouragement. Ask them how they did it.

Points to Consider

- How might support groups be helpful to teens of divorce?

- Do you think going to a counselor is a sign of strength or weakness? Explain.

- Say you're afraid of getting hurt in a relationship with someone. How could you lessen the fear?

- You can help a friend whose parents are divorcing.

- Organizations exist to help teens deal with their parents' divorce. This book lists some of them.

- Successfully coping with divorce makes teens stronger, more capable, and ready to move on with their life.

How to Help a Friend

If you have a friend whose parents are getting divorced, that friend may need your help. Everyone's situation is different. But usually every person has feelings of anger and loss. Sometimes just being there is the best thing you can do. But don't pressure the friend to talk. He or she may not feel comfortable talking. Let your friend know you are okay with that. Wait for your friend to tell you what she or he wants. Eventually, your friend may be ready to talk.

At a Glance

Here are some ways you can tell if friends need help coping with divorce:

- Their grades drop or they begin to have other problems at school.

- They're angry and hostile.

- They fight with friends, brothers, or sisters.

- They blame themselves for problems arising from the divorce.

- They have difficulty concentrating.

- They seem depressed or withdrawn.

"Will My Parents Divorce, Too?"

If you see a friend's parents divorcing, you might fear that your parents will divorce. It may make you feel scared to help. However, if a friend's parents are divorcing, that friend may need extra support. Helping a friend whose parents are divorcing can be hard. But it also can make your friendship much stronger.

Helping a Friend Face a Divorce

Most divorces are upsetting to the teens involved. Encourage your friend to get help in dealing with the anger and confusing emotions he or she may feel. Suggest talking with a professional who is trained in helping teens. Suggest joining a support group. You also may want to give a friend this book.

Before 1960, about 11 percent of children experienced divorce. That number had increased to about 33 percent by 1980.

Rosemarie, Age 15

Rosemarie's best friend, Lily, was staying at Rosemarie's house. As the two got ready for bed, Rosemarie noticed Lily was crying. "What's wrong, Lily?" Rosemarie asked.

"Nothing," Lily said. "I don't want to talk about it." She crawled under the covers.

Lily's parents were divorcing. Rosemarie's parents divorced five years ago. Rosemarie thought she could help Lily get through it. It was hard because Lily didn't like to talk about it. Rosemarie tried to be sensitive to her friend's needs. She didn't push.

Rosemarie did suggest to Lily that she see a counselor, but Lily wasn't ready. Rosemarie decided to back off for a while. Instead, she just let Lily know she was there to listen.

Rosemarie said, "Okay. Goodnight, Lily. But remember I'm here to talk if you change your mind."

Advice From Teens

Chad, Age 18

Chad was graduating from high school that evening. He put on his cap and gown and looked at himself in the mirror. He liked what he saw.

It was five years since Chad's parents got divorced. His relationship with his mother was better. And he was starting to renew a relationship with his dad. A friend of Chad's whose parents just got divorced once asked him, "How do you deal with it?"

Chad told his friend honestly, "You just wake up and try not to take anything for granted."

How Other Teens Have Dealt With Divorce

Surviving a divorce can make teens stronger. They can end up feeling like Rosemarie and Chad.

Rosemarie feels strong since her parents' divorce. She feels she can help Lily. Rosemarie feels like she is better prepared to deal with just about anything that comes up in life.

Chad thinks both good and bad things came out of his parents' divorce. It makes him appreciate things more. He sees how fast life can change. But it also makes him feel unsure. Still, he's happier today than he was a few years ago. He feels a new self-confidence. The future looks good. He's looking forward to the rest of his life.

Rosemarie's Advice for Teens

- Be open to your feelings. Talk with people you trust when you need help working through your feelings.

- Don't burn yourself out by taking on too many activities.

- Listen to what your parents are saying, but don't lose your own opinion.

- Be open to change. Be open to traveling back and forth between two parents. Be open to having two homes.

- Don't feel overly sorry for yourself about the divorce.

- Don't let your parents try to buy your love with gifts and trips. Instead, try asking them to spend time with you.

- If you don't want to talk, get information from other sources. For example, go to the library for books or magazine articles. Then use the information in them if it works for you.

- Don't think divorce can't happen to you.

- Laughter helps. Be as positive about the divorce as you can.

Chad's Advice for Teens

- Talk with someone who has been through a divorce. Sharing the feelings about divorce can help you get through it.

- Life won't be terrible forever. Try to stay cheerful about the future. Believe that if today is bad, tomorrow will be better.

- Read books or take a class on divorce.

- Remember that everyone deals with divorce in his or her own way.

- Think about getting counseling.

- Tell your parents you want to know why the divorce happened, even if the truth is painful.

- Take your recovery one day at a time.

Points to Consider

- Can you learn anything from divorce? Explain.

- List all the trusted adults you know who could recommend help for a friend whose parents are divorcing.

- Which piece of advice from Chad do you think would be most helpful to a friend who experiences divorce? Why?

Note

At publication, all resources listed here were accurate and appropriate to the topics covered in this book. Addresses and phone numbers may change. When visiting Internet sites and links, use good judgment. Remember, never give personal information over the Internet.

Internet Sites

Canada's SchoolNet
www.acjnet.org/youthfaq/divorce.html
Questions and answers about legal aspects of divorce in Canada

Divorce Support for Kids Only!
www.divorcesupport.about.com/people/
divorcesupport/msubkids.htm
Links and articles for teens about divorce and how it affects them

A Kids' Guide to Divorce
http://KidsHealth.org/kid/feeling/divorce.html
Article about divorce in easy-to-understand language

Midland County Friend of the Court
www.midlandcounty.org/foc/stat.htm
Divorce statistics online

Hot Lines

Youth Crisis Hot Line
1-800-448-4663

Covenant House Nineline
www.covenanthouse.org
1-800-999-9999

National Child Abuse Hot Line
1-800-4-A-CHILD (1-800-422-4453)

Useful Addresses

Children's Rights Council
300 I Street Northeast
Suite 401
Washington, DC 20002
www.vix.com/crc
Information to help kids have contact with
parents and family

National Association of Social Workers
750 First Street Northeast
Suite 700
Washington, DC 20002-4241
1-800-638-8799
www.naswdc.org
Resources to help families

Stepfamily Foundation, Inc.
333 West End Avenue
New York, NY 10023
www.stepfamily.org
Information on stepfamily living

For Further Reading

Kuehn, Eileen. *Loss: Understanding the Emptiness.* Mankato, MN: Capstone,
2001.

Moser, Adolph. *Don't Fall Apart on Saturdays!: The Children's Divorce-Survival
Book.* Kansas City: Landmark Editions, 2000.

Sanders, Pete, and Steve Myers. *Divorce and Separation.* Brookfield, CT:
Copper Beech, 1997.

Stern, Zoe, and Evan Stern, with Ellen S. Stern. *Divorce Is Not the End of the
World: Zoe's and Evan's Coping Guide for Kids.* Berkeley, CA: Tricycle
Press, 1997.

Glossary

alimony (AL-uh-moh-nee)—money one spouse pays another for living expenses after a divorce or separation

blended family (BLEN-duhd FAM-uh-lee)—a new family created through the marriage of two people who already have children; a blended family is sometimes called a stepfamily.

child support (CHILDE suh-PORT)—money one divorced parent pays the custodial parent to care for children

conflict resolution (KON-flict reh-zuh-LOO-shuhn)—a way to solve disagreements by negotiating issues in a positive manner

contested divorce (kuhn-TESS-tuhd di-VORSS)—when two divorcing parents can't agree on the division of their property and the care of their children

custodial parent (kuhss-TOH-dee-uhl PAIR-uhnt)—a parent who is the primary caregiver for a child and with whom the child lives

custody (KUHSS-tuh-dee)—legal responsibility to care for a child

family court (FAM-uh-lee KORT)—a setting in which a judge decides the division of property and custody of children

negotiate (nuh-GO-shee-ate)—to solve a disagreement by talking over and agreeing on terms that both parties accept

stepparent (STEP-pair-uhnt)—new spouse of one's parent by a later marriage

uncontested divorce (uhn-kuhn-TESS-tuhd di-VORSS)—a divorce in which both partners agree on the division of property and the care of children

visitation (viz-uh-TAY-shuhn)—time a child spends with the noncustodial parent

Index

Index